# A
# HANDBOOK
# on
# HOPE

Fusing
Optimism and
Action

........................

As told through JOHN McKIBBIN
to GATES McKIBBIN

LIFELINES LIBRARY

For information, contact:

Field Flowers, Inc.

641 Healdsburg Avenue
Healdsburg, CA 95448
707 433 9771
www.fieldflowers.com
www.lifelineslibrary.com

Cover and text design by Kajun Design

Front cover detail from "Emilie Flöge"
by Gustav Klimt (Erich Lessing/Art Resource)

Author's photo by Christina Schmidhofer

ISBN  1-929799-03-9

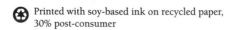 Printed with soy-based ink on recycled paper,
30% post-consumer

*To the angels in my life, be they spirits or spirited friends, who live joyfully in light and love*

Also by Gates McKibbin:

The Light in the Living Room: Dad's Messages from the Other Side

LoveLines: Notes on Loving and Being Loved

A Course in Courage: Disarming the Darkness with Strength of Heart

The Life of the Soul: The Path of Spirit in Your Lifetimes

Available Wisdom: Insights from Beyond the Third Dimension

What began three years ago as a series of journal entries is now coming into the world as a series of books. All along the way people with the perspective and expertise I needed crossed my path at exactly the right time. Each person has contributed soul and substance to the project. I am abundantly grateful to:

♦ **Ned Engle**, who saw what my writings could become long before I did and then adroitly guided me there.

♦ **Barbra Dillenger, Michael Makay, Benjo Masilungan** and **Anthony Corso**, whose comments on each new manuscript reassured me of the accuracy and usefulness of the material.

♦ **Judith Appelbaum** and **Florence Janovic** at Sensible Solutions, whose savvy counsel about the publishing industry kept me confident and on course.

♦ **Carol Fall**, who offered discerning marketing advice and was the creative force behind the book titles.

♦ **Erin Blackwell, Sue Hecht** and **Cynthia Rubin**, whose editorial finesse honored and strengthened the messages.

♦ **Laurie Smith** and **Pat Koren** at Kajun Design, who transformed each book into a jewel within and without.

# CONTENTS

# GLOSSARY

Creation consists of multiple dimensions of reality. Each dimension is characterized by its vibratory or magnetic quality. The higher the frequency at which the dimension vibrates, the more at one it is with God. The **higher realms** are the dimensions of spiritual reality beyond the material world, where distinctions based on time and space do not exist.

**Karma** is composed of imprints on your soul created by your choices (thoughts, words and actions). Choices that embrace spirit heal, balance, complete and remove karmic imprints from your current and prior lifetimes that distance your soul from God. Choices that deny or avoid spirit add new imprints that must be healed, balanced, completed and removed later.

Your **lesson** is the larger karmic pattern or theme you are addressing during this lifetime.

Your **mission** is the major contribution you are making in this lifetime to enable the evolution of collective consciousness toward oneness with God.

Your **soul** is the vessel for your spirit. It carries an

infinite variety of karmic imprints that record the experiences your spirit has had, in and out of embodiment. Your soul is all love and light. It represents your limitless potential to embrace spirit to the fullest capacity.

**Spirit guides** are spiritual entities who have committed to helping you follow the path of love and contribute to the spiritual evolution of all creation. They whisper in your ear telepathically. They send you insights and intuitive flashes. They reaffirm your deepest inner knowing that there is a benevolent higher power inherent in all things.

The **third dimension** is the material reality on planet earth. It consists of dense physical matter that vibrates slowly. The third dimension is characterized by segmented linear time (past, present and future) and compartmentalized space (measurements, boundaries and separation).

The **veil** is a magnetic field surrounding planet earth that separates the vibratory capacity of the third dimension from that of the higher realms. It forms a barrier between your earthly awareness and your higher consciousness. The veil creates the illusion that material reality—and your survival in it—is your reason for being.

The term **we** that is used throughout this book refers to John McKibbin, the spirit who was Gates' father in this lifetime, and the other spiritual entities collaborating with him on the messages he sent down to her.

# The FACETS
# of HOPE

These messages were sent to me from the spiritual realms by my deceased father, John McKibbin. They started arriving soon after I had completed a volume of messages entitled *A Course in Courage*. These two books complement one another. Whereas *A Course in Courage* focuses on how to utilize light and love to disarm darkness, this book explains how two aspects of light—optimism and action—invigorate hope.

People are naturally inclined to hope. The source of its magnetism is spirit.

We all want to reaffirm that our existence has meaning. We remain hopeful that at the end of the day—at the end of our lives—we will be able to say that we made a difference. The desire to make a difference is spirit-based. Its foundation is the hope that we can each leave the world a little better than it was when we arrived.

Consider the following:

♦ What is your fondest hope, and how are you making it happen?

♦ What is your impossible dream, and how are you

bringing it about, even though it is impossible?

◆ Whom do you love the most, and how are you expressing that love?

◆ Whom do you love the least, and how are you endeavoring to love that person more?

◆ What is your biggest challenge, and how are you addressing it with confidence and courage?

This book will help you reflect on these questions. It offers you guidance on how to be more hopeful in these areas of your existence:

◆ Yourself

◆ Your most intimate relationships

◆ Your friends and family

◆ Your work

◆ Your community

◆ Your spirit

You are blessed in all of these facets of your life. You are loved beyond measure.

May the messages in this book enable you to receive that love with an open heart and share it abundantly.

◆

*Like fire, hope burns with*
*the fames of a passionate belief in*
*a spirited present and future.*
*Like fire, its heat*
*warms the soul. Its light is a beacon*
*for pilgrims on the path to spirit.*
*The flames of the material world devour*
*whatever is within reach of*
*their flickering fingers and leave*
*a trail of spent fuel in their path.*
*But the fires of the spirit*
*burn into infinity.*

◆

# CORRESPONDENCE

This book is a form of correspondence between you and your spirit guides. The word *correspondence* emphasizes the fact that this is not and never was a one-way communication. We are not sending down words for you to read and consider so that we can then walk away from the process. We are deeply involved with you in all aspects of your life.

We are engaged in a dynamic dialogue with you, full of barriers and breakthroughs, chasms and crests. You may be unaware of how we communicate with you, and how often, but we do.

We want you to play a more active role in this correspondence. Talk out loud to us whenever you want. Discuss provocative ideas with friends. (We will hear you.) Tell us when you are confused or at a loss as to how to bring hope into your life. Get angry with us if you want. You will not hurt our feelings. Lean on us for sustenance and inspiration. Depend on us to be loyal and loving.

We ask only that you be as available to us as we are

to you. Thus will our relationship bring mutual joy and, ultimately, hope.

You cannot fail on your journey to spirit if:

♦ You are committed to it.

♦ You desire with all your heart to follow it.

♦ You are patient and persevere.

We are with you.

We will guide you.

We honor your tenuousness and tenacity.

We love you.

# HEAVEN

When we refer to the higher dimensions, we set them apart from the earthly plane. They are different. They are also similar.

Heaven, which is what we call the higher dimensions in this message, is populated by spirits. So is the physical plane. You are, after all, spirit in the flesh. Your earthly challenge is to navigate the obstacles presented by your material existence while you walk the path of spirit.

In heaven there is no material world with its unique provocations. We face similar challenges nonetheless.

All manifestations of spirit are occupied with guiding creation closer and closer to ultimate union with the One. This is an unfathomable task. There are more universes than you can imagine, all of them in varying degrees of oneness with God.

Consciousness of spirit enables beings, even as they are tempted by darkness, to choose love and light. Each time they do, they bring themselves and all of creation closer to the One. Each time they choose darkness, they move themselves and all of creation away from the One.

This dynamic never varies, whether spirit is manifest on earth or in another galaxy, another universe, or in the higher dimensions called heaven. We all exist to pursue the same end, even though the means vary according to each plane of existence.

So the distinctions between heaven and earth are both huge and miniscule. They are huge in that the spirits that reside in heaven are souls unbound by material existence. We can be in many places at once; we can see past, present and future simultaneously; we can communicate through vibration and travel faster than the speed of light. We also have easier access to highly evolved beings because we vibrate at a higher level.

We may have easier access, but we do not have greater access. Spiritual masters from the higher realms are just as available to you as they are to us. We see them at work on planet earth every day, in many locations at once. They are deeply committed to doing everything possible to contribute to your spiritual evolution, as are we.

We are all in this together. We have been from the beginning and will be until the end—when we all are one. There is every reason to hope—and to move together toward that oneness.

# REALITY

Reality is a word that defies straightforward definition. That might seem odd considering that most people believe reality to be more real, and therefore more describable, than many other aspects of life. You tend to perceive reality in third-dimensional terms. The third dimension is your home on planet earth, the one you occupy when your soul takes embodiment. Often you perceive reality in terms of physical dynamics—what occurs when people interact and things intersect. That is your most immediate and factual reality. It is also your most *real* reality. Therefore, you assume that it is the most influential one in your life.

That view of reality is accurate as far as it goes. Other realities exist in other dimensions—dimensions that you also occupy even though you may not be aware of them. Each dimension has its own material reality consisting of energy and magnetic vibration. Each dimension also has a spiritual reality to the degree that spirit can occupy space in that material reality.

In the third dimension, which consists of dense matter, energy vibrates at a lower frequency and moves at a slower pace. Spirit must shift its vibration significantly to live there. Being present within and around such an environment compromises a great deal of spirit's power and effectiveness.

As you move into higher dimensions, which have more etheric realities, you move away from segmented, compartmentalized, material reality and toward a more holistic, energy-based, spirit-infused reality. At the highest dimensions, even light as you know it is almost imperceptible, since the frequency vibrations there are extraordinarily rapid. Although it is the place of apparent nothingness, it is home for all of creation. Paradoxically, what you would see from a material perspective as containing nothing in fact contains everything.

Even while your soul is in embodiment, occupied significantly in the third dimension, it travels between other dimensions as well. You are both matter and spirit, mind and soul, person and God, individual and collective.

You are all of reality—all realities at once.

13

# HOPE

Hope is born of spirit and sustained by optimism and action. It is the rooted faith that no matter how challenging your immediate circumstances, there is a path through and beyond them.

Consider what these two sentences imply:

♦ People face trials in life, some of them quite formidable.

♦ Those trials cannot simply be willed away; rather, they must be addressed realistically.

♦ There is a path that goes through—not around— them and leads to the other side of the problem.

♦ To follow this path, you must take one step, then another; action is required.

♦ The catalyst for each step is faith that spirit will guide your actions, coupled with the confidence that those actions are both possible and potentially effective.

There have been times in your life when your hopes have been idle. You said, "I hope to..." but did nothing. There was no change. Why say such a thing? Hoping without acting does nothing to create a desired reality. Declarations of hope that are unsupported by actions are futile because they ignore the spirit in which true hope dwells.

At other times you said, "There is no hope..." when in actuality there was, but you failed to recognize it or take action toward it. Your statement was an assertion that spirit did not dwell in the circumstances you were facing. That is never the case.

There is always reason to hope. Where there is spirit, there is hope.

Spirit is everywhere. Hope is everywhere as well.

To be hopeful is to reaffirm spirit. To act on hope is to reaffirm your faith in spirit. And to reaffirm your faith in spirit, no matter what external circumstances you face, is to move closer to God.

# HOPEFUL

Most people think of hope as an elusive aspect of their lives—something that comes and goes without warning and over which they have little control. Nothing could be further from the truth.

Hope is a function of your conscious thought and overt actions. You are hopeful when you think positively about a situation and take steps to create it in your life. You are hopeless when you believe that the outcome will be less than what you want. Thus, you take no step toward a more positive result.

You have a hand in constructing most of the circumstances that surround you. Even when you do nothing at all to produce them, your inaction can influence the outcome as much as your active participation.

Furthermore, you cannot create what you cannot envision or what you do not believe is possible. Your thought patterns and attitudes about potentialities in your life can be either catalysts for change or barriers to it.

If you want to nurture hope, fuel your faith that

spirit exists in all situations. If you want to actualize faith in spirit, behave as if your hope were an observable part of your reality and not just an ephemeral wish.

Envision and expect light to radiate from all aspects of your existence. Assume that the light is obvious to everyone. Know that every individual who may influence the matter adopts the belief that, "Well, of course we are aligned in purpose and in love."

Are you thinking, "What a naïve thing to do! How often is that the case? I would be steamrollered if I took that stance under some circumstances."? Such thoughts leave you less hopeful than you could be.

Believe the following: Love exists everywhere because God is everywhere. Your material reality may make it more difficult to recognize that love is there, but it does not obliterate the presence of love. It just veils it. There is a big difference between removing and obscuring spirit.

To assume that love is present in every case is not naïve. Love arises from the most palpable reality: the presence of God. Love does not make you vulnerable; it enhances your strength and influence. To love when others do not is to recognize spirit where others do not. To act from a base of love when others do not is to see God where others do not.

To act from a base of love is to be hopeful when others are hopeless.

# METHODOLOGY

How is scientific methodology related to hope? Hope becomes a reality when you follow definite steps toward your goal. However, they are effective only if your intentions are born in spirit.

What is the methodology of hope? It has a number of components, each of which is absolutely essential to the maintenance and materialization of hope.

♦ Find time to understand the higher purpose you want to accomplish with each day, with each year, with your life.

♦ Understand that this higher purpose requires you to be love and light all of the time—not just when you are full of energy and optimism and not just when it suits your mood. All of the time.

♦ Determine what you need in order to fulfill that higher purpose. What do you currently have going for you? What do you lack? How can you mend the tatters and fill the gaps?

♦ If it isn't all the time, then your definition of purpose may not be high enough. Elevate it. What could you do with your life if you were all spirit? Who would you be? How would you approach situations? What would you embrace? What would you avoid?

♦ Commit to that higher purpose. Recognize all of the little, almost imperceptible ways in which you can act on that purpose every day, in every interaction—whatever you are doing, whoever you are with.

♦ Affirm that if that is your intention, you will have the capability, commitment and resources to achieve it.

♦ Stay the course of your higher purpose. Yes, you may be pulled from it or led to believe you are on it when you are actually drawn to less valid objectives. You are human if you get off course. You are spirit if you choose to get back on it.

♦ Allow spirit to energize and guide you, to fill you with assurance and move you with optimism. Enable spirit to flow to you through both victories and defeats.

♦ Remember, spirit provides the wings of hope; your mind and body provide the grounding and traction. You need all three, all of the time.

♦ Attaining your higher purpose requires faith and action, intention and attention, prayers and pragmatism.

♦ When you realize your purpose, recognize the role you played. And rejoice, for you will have achieved your mission in this embodiment.

You are a vessel and a vehicle for God's love and work. You are a companion to love and a counselor to light. You give hope meaning.

# OPTIMISM

Optimism in its truest form is founded in the faith that whatever occurs is part of a larger spiritual context. This understanding gives you the ability to see beyond the immediate situation, which may be far from agreeable and not a cause for optimism. It also enables you to remain steadfast in the face of change, when you are being tossed about between apparently positive and negative events.

Optimism is not a function of having things go well. If it were dependent on good fortune, it would be hollow indeed. Nor is optimism the superficial display of positive pretense and good cheer when inwardly you are feeling the opposite. That optimism is shallow, if it exists to any degree at all.

Two people can experience the same set of circumstances and emerge from them one a pessimist and one an optimist. It all depends on how they perceive both what is going on and the broader context in which it is being played out. One person may notice only what is wrong or what could go wrong. The other may focus on what is working or has the potential of working. If you follow what each person envisions based on the same data or input, you will see that one spells failure and the other success.

If that is the case, then you may think that optimism and pessimism are a function of perception, not spirit. But what makes a person optimistic or pessimistic? Fundamentally it is habit—the habit of making sense of what is occurring by using assumptions that are either spirit-based or not.

+ In conversations do you focus on what is coming to fruition or what is not?

+ Do you worry often about what could go wrong, or do you focus on what is likely to work out well?

+ Are you afraid that you will fail, or do you expect to succeed?

+ Do you affirm your strengths more than your weaknesses?

+ Do you see the accomplishment of your goal as being a process of small successes, or do you envision it as being marked by pitfalls and potholes?

+ Do you see yourself thriving or surviving?

The first step in moving closer to optimism is to pay attention to your habitual ways of thinking, perceiving and conversing. Do they lean more toward optimism or pessimism? We are not suggesting that you refuse to acknowledge problems or issues when they arise and therefore leave them unsolved. Of course you must handle them.

The issue is not whether you see the reality of every situation, but what you do with that information when you get it. Does it make you try harder to succeed, or give up in fear? Do you move forward or protect yourself by avoiding risk?

Optimism is composed of many instances every day when you respond to the circumstances you face with realism and positive thoughts, words and actions. Optimism begets more optimism just as pessimism begets pessimism. Even so, if you have a pattern of pessimism that you want to reverse, you can consciously choose optimism.

Which do you prefer?

# CONFIDENCE

Confidence is different from optimism. Optimism is an attitude, a frame of mind, a set of assumptions about how the world works. Confidence, on the other hand, is related to your own perceived and actual ability to achieve your desired ends. You are confident when you believe without reservation that you will succeed at the task or opportunity at hand.

Confidence, then, is all about you—what you believe about yourself, assume about yourself and honor within yourself. It is supported by other internal and external capabilities you may have, especially competence, insight, fortitude and grace.

♦ *Competence* derives from your skill, knowledge and experience.

♦ *Insight* emerges from your ability to perceive many perspectives from within.

♦ *Fortitude* gives you the energy, perseverance and faith to continue without regard to the circumstances.

♦ *Grace* is the spirit that lives within you, guides

you, comforts you through your trials and adds to the joy of your accomplishments.

You lack confidence when you are aware that one or a number of these qualities are weak within you. If this self-perception is accurate, it can be quite useful. You need not always be confident.

In fact, lack of confidence can be a good indicator that you may not be ready to embark on a new venture. Why is that?

♦ To have confidence without *competence* is to be naïve about your inability to achieve what you intend.

♦ To have confidence without *insight* is to risk accomplishing an inappropriate goal.

♦ To be confident but lack *fortitude* is to risk stalling midway or worse, enlarging the repercussions of your failure.

♦ To have confidence without *grace* is to succeed in a spiritual vacuum.

Compare your confidence to these four qualities. As you build each one of them you will also gain confidence—the kind of confidence that will help you achieve truly spirit-based ends.

# MIRACLES

People acknowledge the intervention of spirit in their daily lives by labeling some occurrences miracles. Perhaps a person is desperately ill and overnight she recovers completely. It is said to be a miraculous recovery. Or one car comes careening towards another, then at the last minute spins off its collision course. The fact that an imminent crash was averted is labeled a miracle.

You may not be able to point to a particular event in your life that you would call a miracle as defined by the above situations, but miracles bless you all the time. You decide that you are ready for a career change and out of nowhere you get a phone call that leads to a job offer. You make plans that fall through unexpectedly and at that precise moment another more appropriate opportunity presents itself.

Most people would not label these experiences miracles, for they do not have the feel of otherworldliness. They do not seem to defy ordinary human capability.

There is nothing inaccurate about that perspective. Miracles are indeed occasions that result in something a human alone could not achieve. You may be unaware how frequently spirit touches your life, helping you accomplish things that you could not do by yourself. People tend to take credit for most of what occurs. Or, more accurately stated, their ego takes credit. Their ego rationally says, "I did this, then the following happened." The ego trumpets its success, drowning out the voice of spirit that assisted in the process. People may not be aware of the guidance they received from spirit, but it was there.

Miracles do happen in your life, all the time. Miracles require a complicity between your higher consciousness and the spiritual forces that surround you. This is quite a practical partnership. It is also invisible and to many, unfathomable.

Life is miraculous constantly—not just frequently. You can make miracles happen for yourself and others by:

♦ Seeing spirit in everyone and everything
♦ Applying every ounce of your capability to achieving just, appropriate outcomes through your words and deeds
♦ Opening your heart to the power of spirit
♦ Being grateful for the miracles that grace your life

Mind and spirit, conscious and unconscious thought, intention and action—all are required to create a miracle. And it takes eyes that perceive beyond the obvious to recognize the miracles that surround you.

# FRUITFULNESS

To hope is to be optimistic that your investment of self and spirit will honor God. Fruitfulness, then:

- ♦ Is rooted in hope
- ♦ Requires you to use both self and spirit
- ♦ Accomplishes something that strengthens the God-force on earth

To be fruitful is not to use your power or control to achieve ends that benefit the few over the many. How can it be fruitful to forge ahead selfishly? Can that approach honor spirit? Of course not.

To be fruitful is to prevent harm from replacing the good in any situation. You reaffirm the existence of God when you take action against negative forces that seem to be beyond your control, be they physical, psychological or spiritual. Inaction in such circumstances cannot reaffirm the existence of God.

Fruitfulness results when you reinforce and reaffirm the existence of spirit in your thoughts, words and deeds.

**Thoughts:** Does fruitfulness always require action of some sort? Not necessarily. Actions might seem to be more relevant than thoughts or words because they are more closely connected to the material reality that surrounds you. But your material reality is neither more important nor more relevant than the mental and psychological reality you inhabit.

Fruitful thoughts create the context through which you travel through the day. Your thoughts can be either hopeful or hopeless. Often they are somewhere in between. The more full of hope you are, the more spirit can accompany you.

If your thoughts are rooted in fear, find its source and purge it from your thoughts and beliefs. If you let fear remain, it will become your reality. It will creep into your conversations and actions. You destroy your fruitfulness when you let fear overcome hope.

**Words**: Fruitful words communicate your intention to make spirit more prominent in your life. This involves more than stating your intention, although it never hurts to do that. More important than the words you choose is the message contained in those words. Do you send a message of hope or of despair, of optimism or of pessimism, of can do or can't do?

If you engage in frequent conversations about all of the terrible things that could befall you, your words could not possibly be fruitful, could they?

**Deeds**: Finally, fruitfulness is linked to your deeds. The actions you take must focus on building a material reality that enables you and others to live with spirit.

You may encounter situations of significant inequity and abuse. One person may have more power than another and use it to create greater advantage. Action against the person with power is possible. Inaction is fruitless for both the person in power and the one who is powerless.

When you find yourself in an abusive situation, you can alter the pattern. You understand clearly what is occurring and refuse to reinforce that reality. You act with conviction, even when others do not. Your words are fair, even-handed and compassionate, although they may be the only ones of the kind being uttered.

That is fruitful.

When your thoughts, words and deeds work interdependently to manifest spirit, you cannot avoid a fruitful result.

# MINDFULNESS

You can hope all you want, but if you are not mindful of your attitudes and behaviors, that hope can be negated in an instant.

Mindfulness is your ability to attend to all of the nuances inherent in how you live your daily life. Moment-to-moment you react and feel, decide and profess in ways that either honor spirit or dishonor it.

You are mindful when you can determine the difference between honoring and dishonoring spirit. This requires you to attend to what you think and how you behave from one situation to another, from one breath to the next.

The first step in mindfulness is learning to recognize the difference between times when you are in spirit and times when you are not.

The next step requires you to observe as well as participate in everything you do. When you are talking with others, all of you should be engaged in the conversation. All of you should also be noticing the authenticity and spiritedness with which you approach the encounter.

30

Perhaps you are seeing the world through rose-colored glasses, imposing false beauty and hopefulness on your world. You refuse, consciously or otherwise, to recognize those aspects of a situation that are lacking in spirit. You want to believe that all is well when it is not. When you require that the darker aspects of reality remain hidden, you express a lack of hope that they can be replaced by light.

Isn't it far better to acknowledge the reality of what is, the better to enfold it with your light? When you do that, you take off the rose colored glasses and see with the unfailing, 20/20 vision of mindfulness.

Mindfulness is a means of receiving honest information from yourself about the degree to which you are in spirit. It keeps you from fooling yourself about where you are and what you are really thinking. When you confront yourself in this manner, you learn quickly what mid-course corrections to make. This applies to long-term errors and unexpected frustrations alike.

To be mindful is to align yourself with God's love for you in the most basic way.

# FORTITUDE

To have fortitude is to go forth with energy, perseverance and faith. Consider these three factors:

♦ *Energy* enables you to move with decisiveness and force to achieve your purpose.

♦ *Perseverance* allows you to continue with patience and determination despite setbacks, delays and difficulties.

♦ *Faith* permits you to see the bigger picture and be comforted by your inner knowing that you are spirit and are guided by spirit.

The path to spirit is anything but easy. Those lacking in energy, perseverance and faith will not make much progress. Fortitude is essential if you are to embark on what is truly an heroic journey of spirit.

How do you know beforehand if you will have the fortitude you need? You don't. You must simply take a step forward, then another, then another. Watch what happens, what tests your fortitude and how you react. Are you stronger in one of the three aspects than you are in the other two? If so, depend on that one to keep you going while you consciously develop the others.

Do you wonder when you will arrive at the end of your spiritual journey? If so, realize that it is far, far away from you now. You will pass through more way stations than you can possibly imagine. At each one you can acknowledge your progress, rebuild your energy and reaffirm your perseverance and faith. Then you can move on to the next.

The blessing of fortitude is that when your energy, perseverance and faith grow stronger, your subsequent intentions and actions reinforce the foundation on which fortitude is built. The challenges you face on your path to spirit may increase along the way. But then, so does your fortitude.

You are never given more than you can handle. But you are given exactly as much as you can handle. You are also given the opportunity to build your fortitude, which keeps you going and growing.

# MINIMALISM

Minimalism is an approach to life that emphasizes the fullness of emptiness. A minimalist space has few objects within it, each one enhancing the environment as much by what it does not add as by what it does. Minimalist art and architecture create form out of a spare number of lines and segments, angles and appendages. Minimalism in life celebrates your ability to be satisfied with an abundance of very little.

What does this mean in practical terms? How can you be a minimalist without renouncing all worldly endeavors and becoming a cave-dwelling monk? Isn't that the epitome of minimalism? Yes, it is.

Perhaps you spend much of your free time chatting on the telephone with friends. Some conversations are meaningful. Others meander, leading nowhere in particular. Why not keep the lackadaisical chats to a minimum? You can then invest the time you freed up in something that affords you greater joy or fulfillment.

Simplicity in all aspects of your life is a form of minimalism. First and foremost, simplicity means absence of clutter. Clutter can be any or all of the following: too many people, things, responsibilities or commitments, all of which clamor for your attention and time. Trim them down and you leave time and space to pursue your primary purpose—to live and breathe in spirit.

How can you become more of a minimalist? Assess the following:

♦ Material things
♦ Relationships
♦ Scheduled commitments
♦ Unscheduled time-consuming activities
♦ Responsibilities to yourself and others
♦ Thoughts, feelings and emotions

Now take a look at the items on your list. Get rid of whatever:

♦ You do not need or use
♦ You do not like or no longer want around
♦ Causes the light and love within you to weaken
♦ Introduces darkness into your life
♦ Compromises your integrity
♦ Feeds your ego unnecessarily
♦ Costs you more than it is worth

You'll be amazed at what a minimalist you can become.

# FARSIGHTEDNESS

Farsightedness as we refer to it here is the ability to see potential reality that may be in the distant future but is perceived as eminently attainable nonetheless.

Farsightedness maintains hope by:

♦ Enabling you to transcend any present or future circumstance that could interfere with your envisioning unlimited possibilities.

♦ Empowering you to see how spirit currently and continuously graces your life.

♦ Helping you recognize the larger context in which your life is taking place—the scheme of things that frames the smaller vignettes you experience day-to-day.

♦ Balancing the immediacy of your material existence with the extended reality of your spiritual existence.

The ability to be farsighted, then, strengthens hope in the long term because it helps you recognize that you can move beyond those aspects of your life where spirit is lacking.

Hope necessarily assumes that whatever comes next —whether it is in the next second or the next century— will bring more spirit into your life and into the existence of humankind.

How does farsightedness relate to living in the moment? Aren't they at cross-purposes? Isn't it impossible to live fully in the moment while maintaining a vision of a larger reality for your soul?

No, it is not. It only seems impossible because it is so hard to be both spirit and flesh. When you enter the higher realms, you discover that past, present and future meld into one. Time and space in the material world are replaced by timelessness and spacelessness in the higher dimensions. You can live in the moment and remain farsighted.

Farsightedness enables you to see a future reality laced and graced with spirit. Whenever you engage in farsighted hope, you energize the spiritual potential inherent in each situation. And every time you do that, you move your current reality closer to your envisioned one.

# POETRY

Poetry involves the use of language to create lyrical, metaphorical or abbreviated messages. It is less casual and verbose than conversation. It is less linear than written narrative, yet it can communicate more clearly and concisely.

Poetry uses language not just as a communication tool, but as a vehicle to transport your consciousness to the higher realms. Poetry contains more grace than mundane speech, although everyday language can overflow with grace if the person using it embodies grace.

Poetry strings words together in unique ways that create significance beyond the immediate meaning. Poetry has a message (what the stanzas say) and a meta-message (what the poem implies).

There is poetry in color as well. Mauve, for instance, is a subtle blend of violet and gray. More than any other hue in the spectrum, this one best represents hope.

Violet is the color of spirit. Greatly evolved spiritual entities emanate violet in their auras, as do people who are deeply in touch with spirit.

Gray is the color of the material world. It represents the space between darkness and light, which is the reality of the earthly plane. You breathe and believe, decide and do, amidst shades of gray.

To hope is to combine intention and attention, faith and action, spirit and practicality. To hope is to combine violet and gray in just the right proportions. Too much violet weakens your ability to perceive the most pragmatic path. Too much gray causes spirit to lose its luster and light. But when the two come together to create mauve, there is strength and effectiveness in the hope you experience.

To understand the rhythms, rhymes and colors of life is to affirm the spirit that connects us all.

That is poetry. That is the meta-message of life.

# CULTIVATION

Hope needs to be cultivated as carefully as plants in a well-tended garden. It isn't a seed that you can sow and then forget about. It's not a garden that grows endlessly on its own, blooming fragrant bouquets and spreading its green foliage for all the world to see.

On the contrary, hope is as fragile as it is resilient. It is fragile because it can be extinguished with the slightest gust of fear or foreboding. It is resilient in that it can blossom again despite the severity of the conditions in which it exists.

How do you cultivate hope?

♦ Take care to recognize the workings of spirit in all that surrounds you.

♦ Find time to imagine a benevolent future in all of its aspects.

♦ Take an active role in the creation of a grace-filled reality. Feed your optimism by acknowledging your accomplishments.

♦ Weed out the parasites and predators that crowd out spirit.

+ Enjoy the fruits of your cultivation.
+ Celebrate the glories of God that grace all of existence.
+ Sleep in peace, knowing that by cultivating spirit in yourself and others, you are giving God the greatest gift imaginable.

# FIRE

The balance of nature requires the interplay of the elements fire, earth, air and water. Each is essential to the maintenance of the physical world. Each complements its opposite and integrates with its partners in synergy. Like fire, hope burns with the flames of a passionate belief in a spirited present and future. Like fire, its heat warms the soul. Its light is a beacon for pilgrims on the path to spirit. Without hope—without fire in their consciousness—they would be tempted to give up the journey when it becomes particularly arduous.

The flames of the material world devour whatever is within reach of their flickering fingers and leave a trail of spent fuel in their path. But the fires of the spirit burn into infinity. Their fuel is self-perpetuating, for it is the joy derived from living in the light and sharing unconditional love. Hope energized by light and love cannot be extinguished, nor can light and love depart wherever there is hope.

Notice the fire that burns within you. It may be a tiny flame, so soft as to be almost imperceptible. It may be more like smoldering coals, bright and hot from their having been flames previously. It may be a conflagration, so intense with white-hot knowing that it intimidates others rather than drawing them to your spirit.

Fire consumes, offering heat and light and leaving ashes in its wake. It has the power to transform matter by burning the energy contained within it. It can also cleanse and purify, wiping out the debris and decay that can hinder renewal.

Fire clears the ground for rebirth, although it does so neither subtly nor gently. When you build the flame of spirit within you, much of what is old, familiar and comfortable will be destroyed. There may be a time when the ground lies fallow, waiting for new growth to spring forth.

Eventually, however, the fire will awaken your most profound ability to love and be a humble servant of spirit. That is the blessing hidden in its ashes. Your love is the green burst of growth, arising again and again in the realms of spirit.

# GALLANTRY

Little typifies the blending of optimism and action more than gallantry. To be gallant is:

- ♦ To leap into the unknown with confidence and certainty
- ♦ To defend a purpose you believe in against relentless opposition
- ♦ To be selflessly courageous in achieving a higher purpose

In literature and the media, you hear about heroes and heroines who accomplish incredible goals, but often their purpose is based in ego rather than service. They are focused more on achieving fame and notoriety than they are on helping other people or standing firm for principles they believe in. They may accomplish heroic deeds, but for inappropriate reasons.

Gallantry emerges from a sense of fair play and common good. It nudges people to consider factors that extend beyond their personal gain to build roots of trust and caring deep within a community. The motto for this kind of gallantry is similar to that of the Three Musketeers, but with a twist: One for all and all for *the One*.

The individual who stands firm for the principle of one for all establishes a high standard for others to follow and emulate. When that standard reflects the desire that your actions be for the One—in other words, in service to spirit—the deeds that can result are grand indeed. But when the emphasis is turned in the opposite direction, away from the greater good and toward your own benefit, gallantry is simply greed in disguise.

Gallantry resides in simple acts of graciousness as much as it dwells in larger heroic ones. It involves nothing more, really, than following the Golden Rule: Do unto others as you would have them do unto you.

What could be more gallant, or more aligned with spirit, than that?

# PROGRESS

Just how will you know that you are making progress on the path to spirit? After all, it isn't as obvious as the progress you make walking a long distance, cooking a meal or reading a book. There are no mile markers, recipes, page numbers or chapter headings on this vaguely defined pilgrimage.

To progress is to move forward. The choices you make will move you either closer to spirit or away from it. How can you determine the result of your choices in the higher realms where your soul resides when all you have to go by is what you experience in the material world?

Spiritual progress can be easy to recognize if you know what you are looking for. Put simply, you are making progress if you are experiencing more love in your life. Love manifests in many ways besides the obvious one of a one-to-one relationship.

You are making progress on your path to spirit if:

♦ You are feeling more loving toward others.
♦ Your sense of inner peace is deepening.

- You have flashes of ecstatic joy.
- You experience what unconditional love feels like.
- You imbibe the love flowing to you from others.
- You believe to the depths of your soul—even for a moment—that whatever is, is perfect.
- Your heart experiences deeper empathy with another.
- You notice that you are engaging in more acts of selflessness.
- You are simplifying your life.
- You are speaking and acting with integrity.

That progress is noble in its purity.

# ABUNDANCE

Hope is based on an abundance of spirit, which expresses itself in daily life as generosity, selflessness, caring, forgiveness, compassion and love. Such abundance begets more of the same.

What is currently abundant in your life?

♦ Is it connected with hope or hopelessness?

♦ Does it bring love into your life or hold it at bay?

♦ Does it energize your sense of self or belittle it?

♦ Does it cause you to find joy in the simplest of things or anguish over the complications of life?

Look at the above list again. It will help you determine the type of abundance you have. If your list is infused with light, the abundance that surrounds you will energize your life. If darkness dominates, a shroud of sadness, despair and hopelessness will engulf you.

You can bring light into the places you choose. Indeed, you draw to you many of the dynamics that affect your life. Whether your existence is filled with an abundance of joy or of sorrow is a reflection of you.

Be conscious of the abundance you experience in life.

Create beauty in simplicity. Infuse with your inner light the darkness that visits you. Be kind and gentle with yourself and others. Never fail to honor each individual manifestation of spirit.

That will affirm and renew hope in abundance.

# ENDINGS and BEGINNINGS

Life is replete with endings and beginnings, as all of creation finds itself in an endless cycle of renewal. What people often do not understand, however, is that many apparent endings are not endings at all, but beginnings. The most telling example of an ending that seems to be truly an ending is physical death. The vessel called the body ceases functioning. There is no longer a person with emotions and energy, caring and charisma inside of it. What could constitute a more obvious ending than that?

This way of thinking about life and death is influenced by a number of assumptions:

- The body is the sum total of the individual; when it ceases to function, so does the person.
- Who the person was, is no longer around and must therefore be dead as well.
- Human life has one beginning and one ending, and what came before or follows after is either nonexistent or irrelevant.
- Death is an ending—not a beginning.

All four of these assumptions are inaccurate. If you

believe that death is an ending followed by no further beginnings, you are wrong.

A human being is body, mind and spirit—not just body. When the soul (which is composed of mind and spirit) leaves the physical body upon death, it returns to the realm of spirit and lives on.

- Who the person was, is still around; you just cannot sense that being's more ethereal presence in your earthly dimension.

- Human life is composed of many embodiments, each one involving the rebirth of the soul into a new physical body. In between lifetimes the soul lives on in the higher planes.

- Death is indeed the ending of the soul's sojourn in a particular embodiment. But it is also a beginning of the soul's next journey in the realm of spirit.

Endings make way for new beginnings just as destruction can pave the way for creation. Do not bemoan the loss inherent in endings more than you rejoice at the gift of beginnings. They are both part of the circle of life. Both are gifts from God.

# WHEREWITHAL

How do you attain the wherewithal to follow hope's lead? What resources do you need, be they inner or outer? How expendable are they?

These questions are relevant to how you will meet your needs on your path to spirit. But first, consider something that may seem implausible. If you are truly intent on making spiritual progress, if that is your deepest desire and most fervent hope, then you will have the wherewithal you need. It may not be what you believe you need or in the proportions you believe are necessary. But it will be there nonetheless.

What do you need on your journey to spirit? You might be surprised at how little is actually required:

◆ Material resources in adequate supply to assure your survival in the physical world, such as food, shelter, tools and clothing

◆ Additional goods to enhance the quality of your life and bring you aesthetic pleasure

◆ Time for contemplation and prayer, inner exploration and meditation

- Relationships that help you address your lesson in this lifetime
- Venues to achieve your mission
- The energy and motivation to persevere and progress

Wherewithal, then, consists mostly of opportunities to move closer to spirit—not things to assist you in this process. Most people think it is composed of objects rather than opportunities.

Assess the degree to which you have the wherewithal to pursue your journey of hope.

- Do you have the material resources to meet your basic living requirements? Is anything lacking that might compromise your health and well-being? If there is, how can you assure that your basic needs are met?
- Does your life afford you special pleasures—walks in nature, appreciation of art or music, a chance to create something yourself, whether it is a meal or a memory?
- Do you take time to be alone and quiet, where you can be at peace and experience the love that surrounds you? Are you doing that enough? If so, continue. If not, find more ways to welcome spirit into your life that way.
- Can you identify your lesson—the karmic pattern you most need to heal and complete during this lifetime? If so, how is your lesson challenging you to transcend thoughts and behaviors that limit you? If not, what might your lesson be? What do your key relationships have to teach you?
- Have you identified your mission—the spirit-based

contribution you intend to make with your life? If so, are you pursuing it? If not, what might it be? What would you like it to be? Can you commit to it?

♦ How motivated are you to continue on your path to spirit, even when others around you do not? Do you return to it after unexpected detours? Do you stay the course despite confusion and uncertainty? Do you celebrate often, recognizing simple contributions and significant successes?

This is the raw material of wherewithal. It requires you to establish the basics, build your reserves, clarify your purpose and carry on. If you can do that, you will have the wherewithal you need to address your mission and lesson in partnership with spirit.

# JOY

God loves nothing more than to see you filled with joy. The more joyful you are, the more in tune with spirit you are. If you are weary and tormented all the time, there will be little quarter available for inner peace.

Because you are spirit, you are capable of experiencing the crystalline clarity of the higher dimensions. The reward for your effort is the opportunity to tap into this energy—to experience your extraordinary capacity to overflow with love and be at peace to the depths of your being. When you experience that, you are more at one with God than you have ever been before. You are filled with joy.

Joy is spirit made manifest as human emotion. It is one of the greatest blessings you can receive. Almost more than anything else, it provides you with the clarity and certainty that spirit does exist. That is the source of your faith.

Joy finds its way into your heart whenever you are open enough, uncluttered enough and detached enough to receive it.

♦ You must be *open* to the possibility that spirit is a flame burning within you. Otherwise you will deny its existence even when you experience its presence.

♦ You must keep your head and heart *uncluttered.* If you are preoccupied with an overwhelming array of relationships and responsibilities, material things and immaterial commitments, there will be little room left in your life for spirit.

♦ You must remain *detached* about the ways spirit presents itself in your life. If you pray for proof of the existence of God, or cling to the notion that God should grant you your desires, you distance yourself from the very thing you are trying to grasp. Give up your attachments, and you create a more welcome place within for God.

As you move closer to openness, simplicity and detachment, you begin to experience more and more joy. It may grace you at unexpected moments. It may arrive more predictably, when and where you experience it most often. But when it is within you, in all of its majestic power and beauty, you will know without question that you are filled with God's love.

# CONTENTMENT

You are contented when you recognize that there is little about your life that you would change. When you can say with authenticity, "I have enough, I am fulfilled, I love and am loved"—you are content.

Rarely does contentment result from accumulating material things, amassing a fortune or gaining power over others. For such action is typically motivated by a sense of not having enough.

Nor does contentment arise from actions that feed your ego but are hollow of meaning. For how can such endeavors help you feel fulfilled?

Further, to be unable to give and receive love is to starve the spirit that lives within you. How can you be contented when your spirit is weak and faltering?

Some people can be content with the simplest of pleasures, the briefest moments of delight, the smallest acts of kindness. Others may live on a grand scale, conquering and achieving, but never know contentment.

Contentment, then, is not a matter of doing or having but of being and loving.

57

Ask yourself these questions:

♦ What aspects of your life give you the sweetest contentment?
♦ Do you honor them with all of your heart?
♦ Do you recognize the grace that resides in contented moments?
♦ Are you grateful for the good fortune that surrounds you?

If so, you are likely to grow more and more contented.

Find ways to expand contentment in your life. Surround yourself with people you love and who love you. Spend your time on activities that bring you fulfillment, whether they involve a lengthy project or the twinkle in a baby's eye. Draw contentment to you like a warm blanket on a chilly evening. It becomes you.

# BEAUTY

It is true that beauty is in the eye of the beholder. Beauty is seen through the eyes of love. Wherever you see beauty, whatever it is to you, you are experiencing love. And whenever you are experiencing love, a significant part of your being is aligned with spirit.

Beauty in all of its manifestations is a central component of hope. It brings you into contact with the spiritual essence, which reaffirms hope.

Anything that helps you recognize the spirit inherent in creation will be beautiful to you. And what is beautiful to you is beautiful to spirit as well. You appreciate it together.

Beauty plays different roles in people's lives. For some, beauty is essential to their well-being. They create environments that are lovely to them, whether they are at home, at work or at play. Others pay little attention to it. For them, beauty is something superficial that distracts them.

There is a difference between that beauty and what people do to make themselves beautiful. Usually this involves concealing their flaws and enhancing their assets. Although such attempts to beautify are not inherently wrong, they do not necessarily enhance the beauty we are referring to here.

Spirit has a strong aesthetic component. Just think of the loveliness that surrounds you:

♦ The moon and stars at night
♦ Vast oceans and mountains
♦ A butterfly's wings
♦ A fragrant gardenia

Would God have given birth to all of this if beauty were not central to spirit?

Consider the additional ways people create beauty with their laughter, their communal gatherings, their art and architecture, their tapestries, talismans and table settings. Indeed, beauty is everywhere.

Pay attention to the types of beauty you appreciate most. Is it natural or artificial? Is it whimsical, lyrical or prescribed? Does it constantly surprise and amaze you, or are you bored with it all? Does it touch your heart, or is it something calculated from the head?

Bring beauty into your life in whatever form you appreciate, as long as it enhances your spiritual essence. Love-based beauty inspires and heals, nurtures and renews. Allow it to grace your life. Be thankful for it. Then give it back in whatever form you choose.

# BOUNDARIES

Hopefulness does not obligate you to rush into every situation that arises. You must be selective in what you take on—and know why you are doing it. You must define and set your boundaries meticulously.

Remember, you are one individual in one body. Your time and resources are limited. Time, in particular, is short. So you must make informed choices about the way you travel through your days. How much time do you invest daily in:

♦ Work-related activities?

♦ Contact with family and close friends?

♦ Home maintenance, food preparation and bill paying?

♦ Leisure time, including time for reflection and whatever soothes your soul?

When the sum total of the above is all too much to cope with, you are over-committed.

This is the time to end over-commitment. This does not mean that you assign rigid time limits to each activity or build a fortress around yourself to prevent real world intrusions into your daily routine.

Instead, pay attention to the ways you spend your time, energy and resources. Allot extra time to an important activity by cutting down on the hours you spend on something less important. You can do this every day, moment-by-moment, in the following ways:

- Define the most important matters in your life and reserve the time needed for each.
- Take note of needless tasks you take on and say no when further similar situations arise.
- Identify daily the events, encounters and experiences that make you feel good; do something equally satisfying every day.
- Refuse to squander precious moments of your life on activities that leave you empty; lavish them instead on objectives that leave you enriched.

When you establish your boundaries and make choices that honor them, you honor yourself.

# FORTUNE

An event is fortunate when the results you experience are guided by spirit, and the benefits are spiritual. Thus what may seem to be the least fortuitous thing might actually be the most fortuitous of all.

You spend your days evaluating events, deciding if they are positive or negative, according to the good that they yield for yourself and others. Now it's time to consider how you reach your conclusions.

- Is your definition of a negative outcome based on assumptions of scarcity or abundance?
- Are the positive results more a function of material gain or spiritual growth?
- Is "good" what makes life easier or more fulfilling?
- Do you concentrate on outcomes that are more immediate and short-term or more encompassing and long-term?

Dig deep within yourself to discover authentic answers to these questions. You might find that they vary from situation to situation and follow no predictable pattern. You may realize that they are founded on stable values and beliefs, whether they focus on spiritual plenty or spiritual starvation.

Whatever underlies your sense of what is fortunate, try stepping into the larger aspects of your existence.

♦ What outcomes do you desire for this lifetime? What do you hope to accomplish for yourself and others? What legacy do you want to leave?

♦ What is positive about your life now? What invaluable lessons have you learned? How have you increased your spiritual awareness?

♦ What is negative? Why do you allow it to occupy precious space in your life? What will it take for you to let it go? How soon can you do it?

♦ What are you doing for your own good? To what extent is that good rooted in spirit? How are you contributing to the larger good of all existence?

Your answers to these questions will help you differentiate between what is truly fortunate and what is not. They will also contribute to your ability to enhance your well-being, which is most fortunate indeed.

# GLORY

The Christian religion has a phrase, "Glory be to God in the highest." And that is indeed unsurpassed glory. But God exists in all things. Thus God's glory inheres in all of creation.

When you are too busy or preoccupied to recognize and appreciate this glory, you dishonor God in a way, for you miss many opportunities to be at one with God.

When you are amazed at the astounding glory of something, you align yourself more completely with God. As such alignment grows more compelling, you become more able to assimilate pure love and light.

You have infinite capacity to be love and light. You have infinite capacity to be glorious.

Ask yourself:

- What is there about you that is glorious? It may be your smile, the weavings of color in your hair in the sunlight, your ability to care for another or your generosity. All of those aspects of you are glorious and deserve to be acknowledged.
- What have you surrounded yourself with that is

glorious? What people, sights, sounds and experiences inspire you? How do you affirm and reinforce them?

♦ During what moments do you experience joy, love or elation? What stimulates those feelings? Each time they occur they are glorious because they are God made manifest within you.

Glory abounds in your life—the spectacular pastels of the time just before sunset, the strains of music that transport you to a place beyond yourself, the revelations of a loved one that affirm the mutual trust you share. Even a cat purring on your lap is glorious.

Breathe it in. Love its aesthetic and essential beauty. Bask in it. Become it.

For you—along with everything else—are glorious.

# GIFTS

You have many gifts—capabilities that transcend the ordinary. You also give and receive many gifts, whether they be wrapped and beribboned or sent over the spiritual passageways of love.

The gifts you receive from spirit are available to you at all times. You do not have to wait for a special occasion to come by them. You do not have to look for the delivery truck, and no thank-you note is expected (although your appreciation is always welcome).

You are surrounded by spirit. At the most elemental level everything in your life is spirit. But the meaning here goes beyond that. You also have spirit guides who travel with you wherever you go. They are beings who have committed to helping you follow the path of love and contribute to the spiritual evolution of all creation.

They whisper in your ear telepathically. They send you insights and intuitive flashes. They reaffirm your deepest inner knowing that there is a benevolent higher power inherent in all things. They soothe you with their love when you are bereft, and infuse you with energy when you are exhausted.

Gifts from your spirit guides are well-founded and thoughtfully chosen. Your guides do not have the option of providing you with everything you believe you need, when you think you need it. They must use precise judgment in determining when to intervene and how.

Why are constraints imposed on your spirit guides' ability to assist you? After all, you can use all the help available. And your guides are capable of providing unlimited assistance, even though they may choose not to.

You are in this embodiment for many reasons:

♦ Your desire and commitment to grow spiritually
♦ Ways you can make a difference in the world
♦ Karmic patterns that you want to heal and complete

Gifts from spirit can help you attain these goals, but they do not replace your choices and actions. Your spirit guides cannot serve as stand-ins for you during this lifetime. How would that help you achieve karmic closure or challenge your strength of spirit?

Instead, the gifts from your guides offer sustenance along the way. They provide guideposts but not a map, feedback but no prescriptions, encouragement but no early exit.

# BACKGROUND

In general, people define an individual's background in terms of years already lived during a current embodiment. This is a limited way of thinking. Your background encompasses many lifetimes and many soul-journeys between. For now, we will use the term *background* to refer to this embodiment only.

What do you have in your background that fosters hope or diminishes it? What has happened in your life, and how has each event affected your beliefs about how the world works?

To a certain extent, you are your background, the sum total of your experiences. At the same time, you are not this background at all, for you always have a choice regarding your perception of what you have experienced.

Your background may be one of privilege. How has your privileged life influenced your sense of self, your sense of purpose and your sense of humanity? Has it led you to believe you are better than others and that you deserve more just because you are "you?" Or have you learned that you have more to give than others and that you have a responsibility to do just that? Whatever your answer, this is more a question of who you are than what your background is.

You may have struggled much of your life to overcome severe limitations, to heal deep psychological wounds, to rise above shame and deprivation. As a result, do you face each day with anger? Do you feel that you have been given a raw deal and therefore the world owes you something? Or do you use these experiences as catalysts to relate to others in similar situations, with empathy and compassion? Does your less than privileged background enable you be more expansive in your caring, or are you more grasping and desperate?

You see, then, that you and your background are "figure" on the "ground" of spirit. Whatever you do with your background, however you see it played out in your life, is your responsibility and yours alone.

The stage setting, as in all theater, is static. Your life on that stage is dynamic. Embrace it with gusto and grace.

# FUN

Are you having fun in your life?

Fun lightens the load and energizes spirit. Life is not meant to be something you force yourself to endure in order to have survived it. Rather, life is an epic adventure, a grand experiment, a transformative experience. Implicit in that process is fun.

Consider the times when you have been at play, whether it involved making sand castles, putting together a puzzle or doing your work. How did it make you feel?

- Were you brought closer to joy, or to melancholy?
- Were you satisfied with what you did, or did it feel like a waste of time?
- Did you feel free to experiment, or were you constrained by a structured approach?
- Were you unburdened in the process, or did you keep telling yourself that the results were not perfect enough?

If you were having fun, you will have answered with the first of the two choices.

If you do have fun on a regular basis—not sitting in

front of the television, but joyful, spontaneous, creative, childlike play—congratulations. You are energizing and rejuvenating yourself in one of the most effective ways possible.

If you are not having fun regularly, determine why you are missing such a central balancing element in your life. What is crowding out the fun? How can you make room for more enjoyable activities and events?

Play. Experience the childlike joy of being unencumbered. And do it as often and as completely as you can.

# EFFECTIVENESS

You are probably accustomed to being your most effective when you have the most invested. For instance, you work quite hard to accomplish a goal that will prove your professional competency or parental abilities. In either case you are motivated by your desire to be effective and to be seen by others as effective. You feel that you cannot fail because you would look bad. Your ego could not stand that.

Or, perhaps you believe that you are absolutely right about an issue and those who oppose you are wrong. You do everything possible to prove your point. In this instance your effectiveness is a function of both your desire to do the right thing and your attachment to proving that you are right.

Much of what you accomplish is motivated by attachment. Without attachments you would be lost. You rely on them to stimulate you to take action.

What if you became more detached and then:

♦ Became less ego-driven and more focused on being of service?

♦ Had nothing to prove?

73

- Set aside your need for positive reinforcement?
- Released your hunger to be better than others?
- Refrained from judging your involvement in the circumstances around you?

At first you might seem to have no anchor. Why? Your approach to effectiveness is usually goal-driven because you believe that one outcome is preferable to another. Consider the following:

- What if your goal were as much about being as it is about doing?
- What if you did everything you could to accomplish an objective and then released the outcome to God?
- What if you analyzed your options and also sought guidance from spirit to help you make the most appropriate choices?
- What if you defined effectiveness as your ability to align your actions with spirit?

Any of these approaches are apt to be confusing at first. You will be using both literal, measurable steps and inspired, indescribable ones. Stick with it anyway.

Start with one activity you are engaged in now that is motivated by your ego's need for reinforcement, then transform it into its opposite. The results can be remarkable when:

- You evaluate your effectiveness based on what, why and how you do something.
- You act with generosity of heart and mind.
- You care as much for others' as for your own benefit.
- Your goal is to make a difference rather than a name for yourself.

# FORESTS

You have a saying for people who are so caught up with what is immediately in front of them, they lose sight of the bigger picture. You say they can't see the forest for the trees.

Think of your existence this way: Every day you face many decisions and even more options. You make choices about whom to talk to, how to act, where to invest energy, how to spend time, how to feel or what to think about various circumstances. In addition, your days are becoming more full—not less so.

Your tendency is to go from one thing demanding your immediate attention to the next. Additional priorities are always waiting in the wings. Even if you complete your to-do list, another one emerges to take its place.

You can always choose to do less, to remove the extraneous items from your daily agenda. Indeed, you should do that on a regular basis.

But this message is not so much about how to do less as it is about who you are when you are doing it. Do you see your day as nothing more than an endless series of tasks to be accomplished? Do you then plod through them in a half-hearted, disinterested way? If so, you will end the day frazzled and unfulfilled. The reason? You cannot see the forest for the trees.

You are so focused on the doing that you have lost sight of the being.

- The doing is the trees.
- The being is the forest.

On the other hand, if you accomplish the same set of tasks, but your focus is as much on who you are when you accomplish them as it is on what you accomplish, you will be able to see the forest *and* the trees. You will reaffirm the larger context of your existence—the evolution of your soul—while you address the catalysts for that growth, which are all of the items on your calendar and to-do list.

- The catalysts are the trees.
- The context is the forest.

Remain conscious of the catalysts and the context, the doing and the being, the forest and the trees. It takes both. Every day.

# COURTESY

You equate courtesy with social etiquette, a set of prescribed rules for acceptable behavior. When behavior does nothing more than gloss over an underlying coarseness, it may make interactions a bit more palatable. But it is not courtesy and will do little to enable you to develop genuine relationships.

Authentic courtesy is rooted in a desire to engage in proper behavior as an expression of respect for others. You do not stare at someone with a disfigurement or laugh at another who stumbles. That is improper. It is disrespectful to that person's mind, body and spirit.

Your interaction with others should be based on respect for what you share on the physical or mental plane. You share a spiritual reality as well, and that deserves to be respected in everyone—if not revered.

Courtesy demands you be respectful of others at all times.

- Coughing in someone's face shows disrespect for his physical body.
- Insulting another would constitute mental assault.

77

◆ Forcing your belief system on another would be disrespectful to her deepest inner spirit.

Remember, courtesy motivated by a desire to camouflage your actual feelings or intent dishonors the other's body, mind and spirit. Courtesy motivated by graciousness (grace made manifest) honors another's body, mind and spirit.

Courtesy with grace reaffirms your humanity and that of others. It is always appropriate. Proper regard for the privacy and personal space of another is never futile. Why not give up your seat on the bus to an elderly gentleman? It costs you nothing and would make a world of difference to him.

# SMILE

You can smile through the day or frown through it. The choice is yours.

This may seem like a simplistic viewpoint on a complex set of issues. Objectionable things are occurring all over the world. There are more reasons not to smile than you can name. You could spend an hour listing them and still have only scratched the surface. Yes, a frown would certainly be warranted.

Why smile in the face of all that?

Why not?

You can choose to see only what is wrong, in which case you will be caught in the maelstrom of human frailty. Or you can see what is redeeming about the way people live together as well as the frailty. Given both sides of that reality, you can always find reasons to smile.

Think of what a smile does for others. Even if you say nothing, when you acknowledge another's presence with a look and a smile, you will have connected with another's spirit. More than you might imagine, this connection reaffirms something deep within both of you.

79

# CLEANSING

Think of how you feel after a bath or shower. Whatever you have accumulated during the day is cleared from your body and your psyche. Something similar happens after a good rain. You experience a palpable freshness in the air.

Your body responds to regular acts of cleansing, as does the surface of the planet. What creates such renewal? Is it just that water has been flowing in and around and between the surface of things?

The answer is twofold. One is inherent in the nature of water itself, and the other arises from the nature of flowing water in particular. Water has the unique capacity to find and fill the lowest point, the smallest crevasse, the tiniest opening. The ability of water to do this is its unique strength. Over time water exerts great influence by its presence, unobtrusively or otherwise.

Water also flows along whatever byways it encounters. Flowing water has two primary qualities:

♦ It alters the magnetic energy in the space immediately around it, increasing the negative ions. This energy field calms the psyche and makes it easier for spirit to penetrate the third dimension. It is not an accident that people are more intuitive when they are near moving water, whether it is in the shower or by the ocean.

- Water cuts through whatever it flows over, creating riverbeds and canyon walls by constantly wearing away impeding solids. It opens new paths by working in the depths, not skimming the surface.

The act of cleansing, whether it is your inner self or your external world, is best accomplished if you remember the traits of water.

- Go deep rather than just hitting the high points. This is crucial whether you are cleaning out a dresser drawer or reaching within to forgive another.

- Allow yourself to flow with whatever presents itself. If there are objects or feelings you are ready to discard, sweep them out. Release them; let them float out of your head and your heart like leaves down a river.

- Remember that the cleansing will make more space for spirit to enter your life. It will create room for light to replace darkness and for simplicity to supplant complication.

- Create "negative ions" around you by letting go of negativity before it has a chance to affect you. Then you will not need to cleanse it out of your life later.

# REFLECTION

Water has extraordinary qualities when it flows—cleansing, refreshing and creating new paths for itself

Still water has its own unique quality—still water reflects. Whether you look into a puddle, a pond or a lake with an unruffled surface, inert water presents mirror images of the world in which it stands: clouds idling in a summer sky, stands of stately trees in a valley, a flower-filled meadow.

Water can accomplish its reflections only in the presence of light. One cannot see anything in water in the inkiness of night.

Self-reflection works much the same way. You need a clear inner light to go within yourself and discover what hides there.

How do you manage to create your inner guiding light?

+ First, you must make your mind and body as still as water. Find a peaceful place and go there alone. It can be to your living room sofa or a park bench. Create solitude and stillness. Allow yourself a measure of peace and quiet.

♦ Then notice what you see when you look within. It might be a mountain of frustration that has been building over time. It might also be a beautiful cluster of willow-tree friendships swaying in the breeze. Whatever presents itself to you, notice all of its aspects. Experience its presence and power.

♦ Now see how this aspect is mirrored in your daily life:

How does it most influence your attitudes and actions?

What is your relationship to it?

How does it limit you, and what can you do about it?

How does it support you, and how can you be more grateful for that?

♦ Finally, use this new level of awareness as a beacon of light to help you see more clearly not only what surrounds you, but how you reflect it. Let that light provide the gentle illumination and astute awareness you need to be able to navigate with more spirit in the world. Vow to engage in similar self-reflection as often and as lovingly as you can.

# THUNDER

There is nothing quite like a thunderstorm. It begins with a bolt of lightning—a flash of brilliance that cuts through the sky. Then there is a moment of quiet, followed by a clap of thunder accompanied by vibrations so strong you can feel them in your body. A torrent of rain provides the backdrop for this drama in the sky.

Thunder and lightning are not just a province of nature. People create them as well. You have heard and felt thunderous applause when multitudes of people are moved to express their appreciation, whether it is for a spectacular sports play, a stirring speech or an exquisite piece of music. Lightning is the spark of brilliance that people witnessed together. Many hands clapping create the thunder.

Thunderous human conflicts arise when a mass of furiously swirling emotions has been building. The lightning can come from anywhere, but it usually takes the form of incendiary words or actions. Immediately two groups form: those who agree with something someone said or did, and those who oppose it. The groups pull apart from each other, gaining strength in their separate unified isolation. Then they come together with a clash, involving slogans or swords.

Recognize when patterns of potentially thunderous conflict are forming, then follow these steps:

- Encourage both sides to engage in mutually respectful dialogue or to negotiate mutually beneficial solutions.

- Identify the possible "lightning bolt" people and neutralize their influence before they wreak havoc.

- Refrain from taking sides or supporting one opinion over the other. Your effectiveness is dependent on your ability to remain neutral, which requires you to release the judgments you may be harboring about either side.

- If the situation is beyond your ability to intervene, remove yourself and retire to a safe place.

- Regroup with others who are there with you so that you will be ready to re-engage once the thunder and lightning have passed.

# FRIENDSHIP

You are not alone in the world. Spirits offer you guidance; family and friends provide encouragement. You need support from both: people on the earthly plane and entities in the higher dimensions.

Your spirit guides and teachers are your friends from beyond. They can see your energetic form quite clearly. They hear your spoken words, tap into your thoughts and stimulate your intuitive flashes. They know a great deal about you, even your most hidden secrets, and regard what they know without judging. They send you messages and insights that help you with decisions and actions throughout the day. They do not decide or act for you. They observe and understand, inform and enlighten.

Family members and friends can do the same for you, as you can for them. Take a look at your closest relationships to assess the quality of love and support that you are giving and receiving.

♦ Are you clear about your personal boundaries and those of others, respecting their right to privacy by being available but not bothersome?

- Do you hold others in loving non-judgment, no matter what you know about their failures, weaknesses or vulnerabilities? Do you receive the same in return?
- Do you extend yourself and get unbiased, caring advice that serves no agenda but to inform choices based on integrity?
- Do you feel inspired, energized and optimistic after spending time with each person, or are you disillusioned, exhausted and pessimistic?
- With whom can you share your life's journey, both the victories and the vicissitudes?

Everyone deserves and needs uncompromising support. You have it from the higher dimensions. You can create it in the third dimension. Do this by identifying the handful of people who grace your life and have these characteristics:

- They trust you and you trust them—absolutely.
- You find that you can be your most authentic self with them—and vice versa.
- They challenge you to be all you can be—and still love you even when you are not.

A few of these people may already be close friends and family. Others may be just acquaintances at this time. Cultivate your relationships with these individuals, for you can support and encourage each other in profound ways.

People who you believe to be true friends may not be so at all. If that is the case, choose to spend less of your self in these relationships, for they do not benefit either of you all that much.

Embrace the blessing of having a best friend who

knows you better than anyone, whether that person is a spouse or a sibling, a parent or a member of your extended family. Love and acknowledge your other closest friends as well. They are there for you unconditionally, as are you for them.

# RADIANCE

People use the word *radiant* to characterize strikingly spirited beauty. A bride is radiant in her ivory gown, with her joyful countenance. Nature is radiant as well.

What makes someone or something radiant instead of merely beautiful? The difference lies not so much in outer loveliness as in manifestations of spirit from within. Outer beauty and inner spirit create radiance.

Remember a time when you were radiant—when you felt and looked your best, when you were confident and poised, when you were brimming over with love and good will. How exceptional was that?

You might assume that you can be radiant only on special occasions when you are jubilant and particularly well turned out. No doubt you are radiant then, but why limit your radiance to those times?

You can be radiant all the time. In fact, you should settle for nothing less than radiance all of the time. You might resist this, believing that to do so would require you to spend too much time being preoccupied with how you look.

That it not the case at all. Try this approach:

♦ Make an inventory of what makes you feel good about yourself and what does not. Perhaps for years you have wanted to lose weight, straighten your teeth or change your hairstyle but have not done so, for whatever reason. Decide now either to make a concerted effort to enhance your self-image by making those changes, or accept and love yourself as you are. Undermining yourself because you do not look exactly the way you want to is no longer an option.

♦ Next, go through your closet and discard everything you have that you do not like or that makes you feel uncomfortable. Wear nothing that reinforces a negative self-image. Instead, wear clothing that makes you feel great, and purchase only those items that will help you feel even better. You do not need a large assortment, but you must love everything you have—even if it is simple and inexpensive. This is not about cost; it is about quality in relation to yourself.

Once you have fine-tuned your external presentation of self, assess your internal sense of self. This is the other—and more important—half of the equation. For you cannot be radiant if you are unhappy, angry or afraid.

♦ Identify what gives you the greatest joy and bring more of that into your life.

♦ Pinpoint the things that limit you the most and address them. It may take a long while to handle them, but start now. Knowing that you are making progress will energize your sense of self—and your spirit.

- Create more opportunities for play and humor in your life. There is nothing like lightheartedness to add sparkle to your smile and anticipation to your step.

Then do one final thing. The next time you are getting ready to leave home to go on an errand, stop and ask yourself, "What would it take for me to be radiant when I leave?" Then make it happen by:

- Putting on your favorite pair of jeans
- Filling your heart with gratitude for a simple blessing in your life
- Anticipating a special treat that you will give yourself
- Smiling at the first person you meet

You may only be on your way to the grocery store, but you can still be radiant.

# CHILDREN

One of the most profound sources of hope is generational. Even if you feel that your own generation and the one that preceded yours has been less than loving, compassionate and responsible, you hope that the one coming up will make up for what your contemporaries created—or destroyed.

There is every reason to be hopeful about what children will do when they grow into adulthood. When they are young, they exist outside the constraints of adulthood, with its power plays and overwhelming egos. Their innocence and untrammeled delight are a wonder and an inspiration.

What is the source of childlike innocence? It derives from unquestioning faith in others and unblocked ability to be at one with spirit. You can see it in the eyes of babies—that Buddha-like peacefulness combined with unreserved trust. Children also have the ability to be totally involved in whatever is happening at the moment, even if the moment is short-lived.

What causes children's initial curiosity and creativity

to erode into control and compulsiveness as adults? Two things occur in a synergistic way:

- ♦ First, children begin to lose their innocence as they interact with the adult world. Some lose it very early. Others lose it during or after they have completed adolescence. Their childlike perspectives succumb to more realistic ones as defined by the adults and older children around them.

- ♦ Second, children bring an awareness of their past incarnations into this lifetime, but that awareness is unaccompanied by the maturity required to comprehend the karmic patterns they must complete and heal. As they grow older, the pressures to deal with this karma become more insistent. Dysfunctional or even destructive relationships, problematic partnerships and difficult decisions manifest. The challenges of dealing with karma lead to the loss of any residual innocence.

Nonetheless, an adult can recapture a measure of childlike innocence. To do so is not to opt for naivete. Rather, it involves:

- ♦ The reaffirmation of spirit amidst those who would suffocate it
- ♦ The choice to laugh at mistakes instead of finding fault with yourself or others
- ♦ The decision to trust in the human spirit even when people prove to be untrustworthy

Children do represent hope and redemption. Perhaps the next generation will, indeed, move the planet toward a more spirited and loving environment in which all of creation may grow and prosper.

More important, however, is the contribution you

can still make as an adult. How do you go about it? You can integrate the most liberated and liberating qualities that you left behind as a child with the wisdom and enlightenment you derive from your experience as an adult. Child and adult together bring out the best in you.

# GRADUATION

To graduate is to complete a cycle of learning and growth that prepares you to for further development at a more advanced level. Graduation itself celebrates your accomplishment while acknowledging your readiness for further experience and responsibility.

Many years may have passed since you attended an official graduation honoring your achievements. Most likely you are due for another one, even though it might be unofficial. How will you know if you are ready to graduate? Here are a few questions to help you determine if you have made the grade:

- What valuable lessons have you learned?
- What did you believe to be true that you now realize is not the case at all?
- How does your inner knowing reaffirm the role of spirit in guiding your life?
- What could you share with others that would enhance their lives?
- Are you more competent in addressing challenges with courage and self-confidence?

♦ Do you appreciate your unique physical, mental and spiritual capabilities?

You do not have to record stellar achievements in all of these areas to be ready for graduation. After all, only one person can graduate at the top of the class.

Commemorate how far you have come as well as the effort, diligence and commitment it took to get where you are. Celebrate your ability to live with grace and good humor—not all of the time, certainly, but a great deal of the time, at least.

Now, decide that you will hold a private graduation ceremony for yourself. It can be as elaborate or as simple as you want.

♦ Will you receive special honors?

♦ Whom do you want to thank for supporting your learning process?

♦ What would you choose to tell others in your valedictory?

♦ What is on the horizon for you?

# EASE

The distinction between easy and difficult is a tricky one. On the one hand, life is full of twists and turns that are far from easy to navigate. On the other hand, an inability or unwillingness to access spirit makes each day much more difficult than it need be.

Life is not easy, but it does not have to be as unwieldy as you tend to make it.

Let's say that you are facing an ethical dilemma. The situation is complicated, and if there is a right answer you cannot recognize it. You are surrounded by shades of gray. Every time a possible solution presents itself, your response is, "It depends."

So you struggle. You lose sleep; you ask others what they would do; you experiment with thinking through different choices; you procrastinate, then blame yourself for doing so.

This isn't easy! But it doesn't have to be so difficult, either.

Your ability to see multiple perspectives and to recognize the potential legitimacy of each option is a strength.

But it should not paralyze you in the process. What else can you do? Where else can you turn?

You can go within yourself. Your best counsel may reside there.

♦ Start first with the issue that resists resolution. What is it, really? Are you searching for a solution to the wrong problem? How can you determine that? Write down the quandary you face. Begin to list, as rapidly as possible, all of the unsolved questions that underlie the dilemma. Write until it feels you have identified them all.

♦ Review the list and select the two or three questions that, if answered, would most help you make a decision.

♦ Write down an answer to each question off the top of your head. You will probably be more on-target than you expect.

♦ Sit quietly and clear your mind. Sweep all of those answers out of your head, but keep the most important questions there. Ask yourself each question and allow your intuition to answer. Your gut-level response is likely to be even more directionally correct than the one you wrote down. Does it feel that way to you?

♦ Acquire information about the questions from knowledgeable individuals and other sources. Take only a brief time to do this.

♦ Review all of the above and see if a pattern emerges that guides you to an answer. If it does not, make your most enlightened choice anyway, but keep it to yourself. Ask your spirit guides out loud for additional insights and information related to that choice. Sleep on it. How does it feel when you wake up? You will know right away if it is what you want to do.

The easiest path through intractable dilemmas involves a combination of rationality and intuition. You need to be intelligent, but you also must listen to your inner knowing. That is the voice of spirit. When you combine intuition with thoughtful reasoning, solutions emerge with greater ease.

# INSPIRATION

Inspiration is lightheartedness combined with joy and inventiveness. The word *inspire* means to infuse a person or situation with spirit. To be inspired is to dwell in spirit.

Inspiration is connected to hope. The two derive from your ability to access the higher power. Hope energizes inspiration. To be hopeful is to see beyond your immediate circumstances and welcome spirit more fully into the fabric of your life.

How can you live an inspired existence? Must you be an accomplished musician or poet, orator or leader to inspire others and be inspired yourself? No, not at all.

Inspiration is easy to recognize when it arrives as a great revelation—an unforeseen insight writ large that takes you to a new level of awareness about an aspect of your life. But inspiration comes in small doses as well, little parcels that arrive daily. Be alert for them.

Perhaps suddenly you think of someone you haven't spoken with in a while and are moved to phone her. You discover that she has become quite ill and could use some cheering up—as well as some chicken soup. That phone call is the result of inspiration.

Maybe you are in a meeting when an idea pops into your head. It seems radical to you because it would take the group in a different direction. But you believe that it has merit, so you mention it anyway. That is inspiration.

Think about what you have done in the past week.

- ◆ Can you identify moments when an idea presented itself unexpectedly?
- ◆ Did you follow up on it? If so, what was the result? If not, why not?
- ◆ Did you discredit it as being invalid? Why did you see it that way?
- ◆ What might you do differently next time?
- ◆ How can you become more aware of inspiration when it occurs?

To be inspired is to be graced by spirit. That is no small matter. Attend to those occasions, for they are boons in unobtrusive packages. They help energize right action and balance your life.

# NURTURING

To nurture is to assist the development of an organism or an idea. Nurturing is different from feeding in this regard:

◆ Feeding provides nutrients or resources for growth.
◆ Nurturing provides sustenance for the spirit that lives within the organism or the idea.

In the same way:

◆ Feeding an individual or an innovation assures that it remains alive because of the intake of food with vitamins and minerals or the allocation of resources such as time and talent.
◆ Nurturing an organism or an idea depends upon caring, which requires you to sense the places where spirit is weak or lacking and strengthen them.

You feed the body.

You nurture the soul.

How do you nurture the soul of an idea? Isn't soul something that only living organisms can have?

Yes and no. Consider the source of an idea, and you

will have your answer. Ideas come from inspiration, which derives from spirit, which dwells in living beings. So to nurture an idea is to identify and care for the aspects of spirit from which it springs.

How do you respect the spirit inherent in an idea? Consider this example. Assume that you are involved with a group of physicians who want to provide free pediatric care one day a month to at the elementary schools in your community. At the planning meeting the group identifies what needs to be done:

- ♦ School administrators must be contacted for their approval.
- ♦ Medical and immunization records must be gathered.
- ♦ A room in each school must be prepared.
- ♦ Arrangements must be made for students to miss class, or to be brought from home if they are very sick.

You decide who will address each need and agree to meet again. At the second meeting people report unanticipated problems:

- ♦ The law precludes providing certain medical services in schools.
- ♦ Malpractice exposure will increase, as will school liability.
- ♦ Many of the schools have no rooms to spare.
- ♦ Medical records are in disarray.

You discuss these obstacles and devise new approaches. But the information people bring to the next meeting is even more disheartening. Your latest efforts have met with more resistance. Most physicians are ready to abandon the idea. You feel powerless to stop them.

Then you realize that everyone has lost sight of the original purpose that inspired these physicians. The group has been so focused on feeding their idea through the accomplishment of tasks, it has forgotten to nurture and reaffirm their shared purpose.

A purpose-driven approach would have attended to both the practical steps that must be taken and the benefits the children would receive once the program is in place. The obstacles the group faced initially would have caused them to regroup and perhaps focus on one or two schools, but not forsake the effort altogether.

Whether the care and feeding is for individuals in your family, plants in your garden or ideas in your community, remember to nurture them as well as to provide resources for their growth. When you do both, you give them every opportunity to develop into even more remarkable creations of spirit.

# SUSTAINABILITY

The issue of sustainability has been at the forefront of ecological discussions for quite some time. How can you preserve the balance of nature while you also continue to grow populations and economies that are dependent on natural resources? You have only begun to scratch the surface in your consideration of workable alternatives.

What underlies this issue? Is it the propensity of people to exert their apparent sovereignty over nature? It is that, and more.

To believe that you are more important than any other aspect of nature is to see yourself at the top of a hierarchy of living species and elements. To perceive that there is a hierarchy at all is to assume that one component of nature is better, more valuable or more influential than another.

But that is impossible for three reasons:
- All of creation is interconnected. What happens to one living thing affects all others.
- Spirit resides in all of creation. Therefore, everything is sacred.

♦ It is not possible to control or destroy spirit.

What creates the need to argue for sustainability? It is the belief that you can do whatever you want to any aspect of nature—people, trees, fish, mountains, mosquitoes—and experience few or no repercussions.

You might argue here that you do have control over a tree. If you want to cut it down, it is powerless to stop you. It will just stand there motionless while you saw its trunk in two and then fell it.

But think of the implications. With that tree gone, there is less oxygen in the earth's atmosphere. When many trees are destroyed, upsetting the atmospheric balance, weather patterns change. This puts crops at risk, making less food available to feed the world's populations.

You know this example well. It has been the source of immeasurable research studies and countless debates. But what is rarely considered in these deliberations is this: Sustainability is possible only when people honor the spirit that exists everywhere and in everything.

To do this does not require you to stop using natural resources. That is impossible. Rather, it asks that you consider that every tree you cut down has a life within it that is similar to your own. You should treat it with the same reverence you accord people.

Doing so would lead you to make more thoughtful decisions about what you need and why. You would acquire less and use less, which would mean that fewer resources would be needed to support your existence.

As more people choose this path, the sustainability of the planet becomes more likely. Equally importantly, they develop and exhibit greater reverence for God.

Sustain spirit with your respect for all of creation.

# ENVISIONING

Whatever you can envision you can create. In fact, the distance between envisioning and manifesting can be short indeed. At times the two occur simultaneously. How is this possible?

In the higher dimensions external reality and consciousness are all but identical. Thus, a thought form is much like its physical representation. A vision is almost synonymous and simultaneous with its manifestation as an event.

People are greatly influenced by the illusion that thoughts are different from things. They believe that thoughts have little relevance to their material existence. The opposite is closer to the truth.

It is imperative that you become more aware of what you are thinking and envisioning with your thoughts. This requires you to be more fully conscious as you go about your daily activities.

Perhaps you are concerned about your financial security. Over the years you have built up a nest egg, but its value is linked with the national and global economy. You read about upheavals in foreign countries and envision the following potentiality:

- The world economy crashes.
- You are left with no cushion of savings.
- Suddenly you become too ill to work.
- You live off the equity in your home, then eventually you have to sell it.
- You end up in a rented apartment, if you are lucky, and on the streets if you are not.

This may seem absurd, but it goes on every day in the minds of many otherwise secure individuals. We are not arguing that because you envision it, such a scenario will occur. We are suggesting that you decipher the aspects of your life that stimulate such a hopeless string of imagined events.

- What are the sources of your fear? In what ways do they overcome your faith?
- Where do you feel most vulnerable? Why?
- What seems out of your control? Is it really?
- How can you change what makes you feel fearful, vulnerable and out-of-control?
- What are your sources of immediate and long-term support?
- What is causing you to focus on your financial security, and how can you address that cause?
- What can you do differently the next time you envision this scenario or a similar one?

Why not envision what you want every chance you get? Imagine what would give you the greatest peace and fulfillment. See yourself contented and complete.

Envision reasons to hope rather than causes for fear.

# ENERGY

You have a finite amount of time each day and must use it wisely. You might believe that the same is true for your energy. Well, it is and isn't.

Although you do need to invest your energy wisely, you actually do have energy in infinite amounts. You just are not aware of all the ways you can access and use it.

You perceive and are taught that your energy supply is mostly physical. If you eat healthy food, exercise, drink plenty of water and get sufficient sleep, you will have energy to do what you need to do throughout the day. If you are particularly tired, you go to bed early. If you are engaged in physical exertion, you eat food to replenish the calories you are burning. You try to achieve homeostasis with your sources and uses of energy. That is good.

You can tap other sources of energy that go far beyond the ones described above. Your mind and spirit can bring forth these resources in remarkable ways.

Think of a time when you had a brainstorm that solved a problem or created a unique opportunity.

Weren't you energized far more than usual? You probably had more vigor than you needed to pursue the idea. This energy spike did not come from shifts in your eating, exercise or sleep patterns. It came from the chemistry in your brain, which was stimulated by something you were excited about.

Sources of energy renewal go beyond mental functioning, however. They are also spiritual. Recall a moment when you strongly felt the presence of spirit. Perhaps it was at a religious service. Maybe it was in the rustling breeze on a hilltop. You sensed a presence and a reality that transcended the physical world around you yet was also integral to it.

♦ You felt it in your body. Perhaps it moved you to tears.

♦ You felt it in your mind. You had an intellectual awareness of this loving force.

♦ As you felt it in your heart, you experienced profound inner peace and abundant love.

♦ After this experience the world seemed different to you. Your worry receded, and you felt more optimistic than before.

You need not wait for spirit to visit you unannounced. You can invite it in at any time. Before you go to sleep, imagine that your body is filled with and surrounded by love and light. If you are tired, ask your spirit guides to help heal and energize your body. If you are distraught, pray for strength and guidance.

The energy released within you as a result may be too subtle for you to feel, but it comes from an infinite source. That energy is by its very nature unlimited. It is available to you in endless supply.

# MUSIC

Treat yourself to as much music as you can, whatever your musical preferences. Enjoying your favorite music is never a waste of time. And you always feel better afterward, don't you?

Why is music so uplifting and renewing? Music shifts the energy in the space it occupies, rearranging the magnetics as it creates each tone. It raises the vibratory frequencies that envelope your environment, thus giving you greater access to the higher consciousness that moves along with those frequencies.

Music has another quality that helps you release negativity. It takes you out of your mind, which may be laden with preoccupations and concerns, and carries you into a place where you are without care. This respite may be only momentary, but it can shift your mindset.

Sing or move along with the music if you want to. The union of your body with the tones and vibrations of the music brings you physically into closer contact with spirit. Have you experienced an eruption of ecstasy while you were dancing or singing—a sense that your body was filled with a different kind of energy that helped you move and sing with more grace and lightness? If so, in those moments you have been physically at one with spirit.

Music brings joy into your life. You cannot have too much of that.

So the next time you have a few minutes to spare, put on a favorite CD. And let yourself fly away with the music. Dance and sing if you wish.

Who knows what you will end up humming the rest of the day?

# VITALITY

The farther along you go on the path to spirit, the more vital you become. This occurs for a number of reasons:

- ◆ You make better choices. You are more conscious of what supports the spirit within you and what stymies it.
- ◆ You surround yourself with people who are on paths similar to yours. You engage in mutual assistance and sustenance.
- ◆ You spend more time in solitude and contemplation. You create an inner dialogue with spirit that informs and guides your daily life.
- ◆ You become more centered on God. You relieve yourself of extraneous concerns and unnecessary confusion.
- ◆ You create a larger space for spirit to live within you. You strengthen your faith and energize your sense of purpose.

Each of these steps activates your vitality as a result of your connection to spirit. And the more vital you feel, the more you can integrate spirit into your life.

The opposite is true as well. There is no hope without a sense of vitality. Hope exists at the intersection of faith and action. Vitality derives from faith and invigorates action.

Take stock of your overall vitality:

+ What aspects of your life replenish your vitality? How?
+ Are there key areas of your life that might be weakening your vitality? Why?
+ What dimensions of your life offer you the most hope? What sources sustain that hope? How can you continue to reaffirm it?
+ Is your faith situational or solid? If it is situational, why?
+ What and where are your doubts? Can they be addressed with respect and honesty?
+ How can you love yourself more?

Enlightened self-love is one of the greatest sources of vitality. The more you love and accept yourself, the more your life will be loving in general and vital in particular.

# WELCOME

We close these messages with a greeting that typically signals arrival rather than departure: Welcome.

We congratulate you on your interest and attention. If you were not committed to the path of spirit, these messages would not have come into your hands. You would not be reading this last page.

You are a keeper of the light. Your responsibility to spirit is to:

- ♦ Carry the flame of love and light with you everywhere—to convey it through darkness and doubt.
- ♦ Love unconditionally in a conditional world, experience oneness where others see polarities, and live and breathe spirit when others around you are living and breathing materialism.
- ♦ Transcend separateness with your generosity and caring.

When you do this, you move rapidly toward spirit, both in the physical dimension and in the higher planes. You are on your way home.

This home is a place of peace where your soul resides.

Here you return when each lifetime is complete. Here you have unconditional support and unencumbered serenity.

It awaits you.

But you need not wait until this lifetime is over to be home. Your spiritual home is available to you now. You can access it with your love. The path has been cleared. The door is open. Your spiritual family is present, anticipating your arrival.

We will assist you on your way and wait for you as long as it takes you to arrive.

We are here to greet you with love, and to embrace you with the words, "Welcome home."

**Gates McKibbin** never imagined that after spending twenty years as a corporate executive, management consultant and adjunct college professor specializing in strategic and organizational renewal, she would publish messages channeled from her deceased father, John McKibbin. For most of her adult life she had balanced a fulfilling professional career and a fascinating spiritual quest. Then quite unexpectedly her father, who visited the earth plane frequently after his death, began sending telepathic messages for her to write in her journal.

Three years and six books later, Gates has now added "Inspirational author and speaker" to her resume. She still helps business executives navigate turbulent change, and she also seeds the planet with insights from the spirit world. To complement the LifeLines Library, Gates has developed a collection of thematic LifeLines note pads featuring her favorite one-liners from the books.

Born and raised in central Illinois, Gates now resides in San Francisco. Whenever she has a few hours of free time, she hunts for vintage jackets, walks to North Beach restaurants for risotto, creates bead-bedecked greeting cards and, of course, continues her journal writing. Gates holds a Ph.D. from the University of Illinois and has received numerous academic awards, among them Phi Beta Kappa.

# LIFELINES LIBRARY ORDER FORM

| Book Title | Quantity | Total Cost |
|---|---|---|
| The Light in the Living Room: Dad's Messages from the Other Side   $9.95 | | |
| LoveLines: Notes on Loving and Being Loved   $9.95 | | |
| A Course in Courage: Disarming the Darkness with Strength of Heart  $9.95 | | |
| A Handbook on Hope: Fusing Optimism and Action   $9.95 | | |
| The Life of the Soul: The Path of Spirit in Your Lifetimes   $9.95 | | |
| Available Wisdom: Insights from Beyond the Third Dimension   $9.95 | | |
| Complete set of six books in the LifeLines Library   $39.95 | | |
| Subtotal | | |
| *CA residents add 7.35% sales tax* | | |
| *Postage and handling (F.O.B.)* | | |
| Total | | |

## Payment Information

Charge to: VISA ☐      MasterCard ☐

Card number _____ Exp. date_____

Ship to:

Name_____

Street_____ Apt._____

City_____ State_____ Zip_____

Phone: _____ Fax_____

E-mail: _____

To order by phone call (707) 433-9771

Fax your order to (707) 433-9772

Order via e-mail at **www.fieldflowers.com**

Visit our Website at **www.lifelineslibrary.com**

# LIFELINES NOTE PADS ORDER FORM

| Note Pads<br>12 messages in each pad, 108 pages | Quantity | Total Cost<br>@ $7.95/pad |
|---|---|---|
| Authenticity (#LL1000) | | |
| Boundaries (#LL1001) | | |
| Change (#LL1002) | | |
| Commitment (#LL1003) | | |
| Companionship (#LL1004) | | |
| Courage (#LL1005) | | |
| Effectiveness (#LL1006) | | |
| Hope (#LL1007) | | |
| Love (#LL1008) | | |
| Real Work (#LL1009) | | |
| Strength (#LL1010) | | |
| Time (#LL1011) | | |
| Unconditional Love (#LL1012) | | |
| Vitality (#LL1013) | | |
| Wisdom (#LL1014) | | |
| Subtotal | | |
| *CA residents add 7.35% sales tax* | | |
| *Postage and handling (F.O.B.)* | | |
| Total | | |

## Payment Information

Charge to: VISA ☐     MasterCard ☐

Card number _____ Exp. date_____

Ship to:

Name_____

Street_____ Apt._____

City_____ State_____ Zip_____

Phone: _____ Fax_____

E-mail: _____

To order by phone call (707) 433-9771

Fax your order to (707) 433-9772

Order via e-mail at **www.fieldflowers.com**

Visit our Website at **www.lifelineslibrary.com**